Prison Segmentation For Detaining Pre-Trial Laptop Workers

Work Instead of Worry

Rev. Mike Wanner

-

Table Of Contents

Introduction

A lot of people in prisons are incarcerated for a long time before they are brought before a judge. During that time their whole life can be decimated by the slow process of jurisprudence.

Incarcerated people cannot support themselves and their families, and that alone can create whole social fabric destruction. When people are starving, neighbors get concerned, and the public welfare people are called upon to help.

A lot has changed regarding portable lifestyles, and I suggest ideas here that can help some of those awaiting trial, their families, and the broader communities.

Earlier I wrote a book called *Prison Segmentation for Defense Support Teams: Can Better Info Help?* Here I would like to take part of that concept further and target a particular segment of the community.

1 - What is a Pre-Trial Laptop Worker

There are many laptop workers in our general society who can work anywhere they have internet access. This segment of the population has the capability of using their computers skills to serve their customers remotely.

I propose here that the judicial system allows special consideration for those who have that Capability. The proposal, of course, would be matched by compensation for the system benefits for the entire community and especially the taxpayers who would otherwise need to pay for everything the prisoner needs to survive.

The benefits to the community would be:
1. First and foremost, the ability of the worker to stay employed or in business so that they can provide for their family.
2. The ability to offset their living expense so the government need not sustain that expense.
3. The maintenance of an income generating option which could be pivotal to their ability to sustain themselves and their families during incarceration and after Re-Entry.
4. The ability of the community to know that the prisoner can sustain their own defense expenses, so there is no likelihood of subsequent claims of inadequate availability of counsel.

5. The ability of the prisoner to earn enough money on their laptops to provide some subsidy to the judicial system in a reasonable and proper way.
6. There may be some employment opportunities which may change the lives of other prisoners elsewhere.

The benefits to the prisoner would be:
1. First and foremost, the ability of the prisoner to stay employed or in business so that they can provide for their family.
2. Second and essential, the ability of the prisoner to stay employed or in business so that they can provide for their defense.
3. The ability to have a significantly better living arrangement than the government would provide by default.
4. The maintenance of an income generating option which could be pivotal to their ability to sustain themselves after Re-Entry.
5. The ability of the prisoner to earn enough money on their laptops to provide a subsidy to the judicial system in a reasonable and proper way so they can optimize their options, choices, and support in general.

2 - Laptop Income Can Influence Options For the Whole System and Country

There was a famous quote from a Philadelphia politician who was criminally charged which was "Money Talks and Bull S___ Walks." The idea was used to describe an illegal activity, but here I suggest that the concept is applied legally.

It is no secret that America is in financial trouble and practical citizens need to be asking the questions about possible resolutions to our problems.

The American system is based on a tradition that was created in earlier times. Options have increased, and practical people can listen to ideas and choose new options.

Technology has helped eliminate the Pony Express, Telegrams, Horse-drawn carriages, and many things that are now called antiques. Technology and common sense can help with the options needed to update incarceration choices.

We need to be risk averse but also practical. Rehabilitation of prisoners is unlikely in the way that they are treated now in many places.

Change can happen, and I am recommending that some ideas of change be considered. Those who are incarcerated but not convicted can have less cost for taxpayers when the prisoners can make choices that do not compromise safety but offer them more options.

3 - Functional Workers with Issues

Many in America can have dysfunctional characteristics but still be able to do what they do in a way that is rewarded by employers and customers. While their life may not be the choice of all others, they may still be able to earn their own way and provide for their families.

Mistakes are made by all kinds of people, and most people make a lot of errors that they get away with, and nobody cares. When someone has an encounter with the police, the issues of yesterday can carry a heavier weight and a process that can impede freedom and ability to function.

The police and the judicial system have their jobs to do so that citizens are protected, and the freedoms are maintained.

The realities of incarceration are that the processes are very complex and the workings take time, and that can be costly in many ways. Many prisoners are parents and the restrictions on prisoners can have significant detrimental effects on their children.

It seems logical to create options that minimize detrimental results to the children. I hope this book can help in that regard.

This book is not advocating totally free (Carte Blanche) web access for those being detained, but it does promote proper career preservation, family support, taxpayer economies and common-sense approaches to detention.

4 - Substance Abuse Detainees

It is not a secret that a lot of the detainees and/or prisoners have issues that may be rooted in substance misuse. When detained, it may be an optimal time for the prisoner to become aware of the need for change in their life.

If the detainee is able to keep their job or business while detained, the income of their laptop lifestyle may make getting help possible and add pressure to the timing.

The society that we all live in is very intense, and everybody can hit a bad patch in the road that knocks them off balance. People can get physically sick and need to go to the hospital for stabilization and a little rehabilitation.

With the stress of our times, it is also easy for people to become emotionally overwhelmed and do stupid things that cause consequences that need treatment.

Independent laptop business owners may be able to justify affording the help they need if they are motivated by the incarceration experience to avoid extending their visit to a destination they did not choose.

Employer Human resources support and union members benefit support could also be options for needed care that can help the detainee stay free of conviction and or a prison record.

In addition to doing right by the detainee, the spouse, children and extended families of the detainees could benefit from not having to endure the emotional and financial costs of having a family member convicted of a crime.

The saving to our society of having the family self-supported in lieu of state-supported could be significant.

5 - Mental Health Detainees

It is also not a secret that some detainees can have issues that may be rooted in mental illness.

When detained, it may be an optimal time for the prisoner to become aware of the need for change in their life.

If the detainee is able to keep their job or business while detained, the income of their laptop lifestyle may make getting help possible and add pressure to the timing.

The society that we all live in is very intense, and everybody can hit a bad patch in the road that knocks them off balance.

People can get physically sick and need to go to the hospital for stabilization and a little rehabilitation.

With the stress of our times, it is also easy for people to mentally act out and become emotionally overwhelmed and do stupid things that cause consequences that need treatment. Employer Human resources support and union member benefit support are much better options for lesser cases than court rulings and prison records.

In addition to doing right by the detainee, the spouse, children and extended families of the detainees could benefit from not having to endure the emotional and financial costs of having a family member incarcerated.

The saving to our society of having the family self-supported in lieu of state-supported could be monumental.

6 - Development Staff Pre-Plan

This idea could be a monumental success or an ultimate disaster. Prior to developing such a concept, it would be helpful for an administration in the jurisdiction to review the longevity of detainees awaiting trial.

Patterns can be used to manage many things efficiently. Jurisdictions with savvy administrators may be able to efficiently determine the likelihood for certain kinds of arrests to result in long-term detention or future release of the detainees.

Of course, the history of detainees would have an enormous determination on the likelihood of conviction. Repeat offenders would be least likely to qualify for the consideration of this particular arrangement so they could be considered later after the success or failure of the idea was evaluated.

Ideally, at some point, the district attorney could be apprised of the findings of administrators, and their recommendations could be invited so as to prepare a balanced efficiency perspective.

Discovered information should be maintained and used to determine candidates for self-sufficient standing if convicted and as early intervention rehabilitation.

If a detainee and or prisoner could keep their computer skills current enough to support themselves, their incarceration and their family, recidivism could be eliminated entirely for laptop workers, and that could help the whole country and the taxpayers thereof.

7 - Planned Levels

Consideration could be given to many levels of capability and work performed. Concept developer should take a look at:

1. Standard accommodation minor upgrades.
   a. Minor Income – little or no extra benefits

2. Substantial accommodation upgrades.
   a. Values scale determination.
   b. Incremental Income and benefits.

3. Major accommodation upgrades
   a. Values scale determination.
   b. Increasing Income and benefits.

4. Awesome accommodation upgrades
   a. Values scale determination.
   b. Increasing Income and benefits.
   c. Family Village configurations.
   d. Business location configurations.

5. Inviting Proposals
   a. Values scale determination.
   b. Increasing Income and benefit.

This idea could be a monumental success or an ultimate disaster. Prior to developing such a concept, it would be helpful for the administration in the jurisdiction to review the longevity of detainees awaiting trial and pick the optimal target audience.

8 - Pattern Planning & Monitoring

Patterns can be used to manage many things efficiently. Jurisdictions with savvy administrators may be able to efficiently determine the likelihood for certain kinds of arrests to result in long-term detention or inevitable release of the detainees.

Of course, the history of detainees would have been a factor in the determination of the likelihood of conviction. Repeat offender would be least likely to qualify for the consideration of the arrangement so they could be considered after the success or failure of the idea was evaluated.

Ideally, at some point, the district attorney could be apprised of the findings of administrators, and their recommendations could be invited so as to prepare a balanced efficiency perspective.

As time goes by, the success of this program could be helpful to trigger the implementation of the principles in my earlier book about *Prison Segmentation for Defense Support Teams: Can Better Info Help?*

Life in prison may seem to be very much about the spiraling down of the life of the prisoners. My books are focused on allowing the direction of the spiral to include up as well.

America is great, and it is vast. If too many people are conditioned to move in only one direction, many lives can be less than optimal.

I hope to point to opportunities that can be done one at a time.

9 - Benefits to Prisoners

1. An opportunity for cost containment that can lead to frugal day to day allocations.

2. An opportunity for revenue to support prisoner benefit programs.

3. A base upon which can be built rethinking of options for prisoners.

4. Something new and different to add to bolster everyday expectations.

5. Opportunity to Rethink real possibilities.

6. Replace standard fixed thinking with Prison Possible thinking.

7. A chance for a Break Through.

8. A chance for Thought Bubble Bursting.

10 - Benefits to Prison Staff

1. Stress reduction from cost containment relaxation that can lead to an environmental upgrade for everybody.

2. An opportunity for revenue to support prisoner benefit programs and reduce angst.

3. A base upon which can be built rethinking of options for prisoners.

4. Something new and different to add to everyday possibilities.

5. An opportunity for Rethinking real possibilities.

6. Replace standard fixed thinking with Prison Possible thinking.

7. A chance for a Break Through.

8. A chance for Thought Bubble Bursting.

11 - Benefit to Taxpayers

1. An opportunity for cost containment that can lead to fewer cost increases and eventual reduction of the day to day financial expenses.

2. An opportunity for revenue to support prisoner benefit programs which can reduce stress on prisoners and by extension prison staff and administration.

3. A resource base upon which can be built rethinking of options for prisoners.

4. Something new and different to add to everyday expectations.

5. An opportunity for Rethinking real possibilities.

6. Replace standard fixed thinking with Prison Possible thinking.

7. A chance for providing a Break Through.

8. A chance to provide a Thought Bubble Bursting.

12 - Street Safety Planning & Monitoring

A reality check awaits those who realize that most prisoners will get out of incarceration someday and they will be free to walk the streets like every other citizen. It makes sense for citizens to be concerned with the way that prisoners are treated and whether they are likely to be ready for freedom.

Unfortunately, it seems that there may be some deficiency in preparation for that event. Being unready may increase the likelihood of failure to find work, and that can trigger recidivism.

The level of recidivism varies by jurisdiction, but the 40% or more may not be unrealistic. In some areas, the numbers can be much higher.

The influence of the laptop workers program may be helpful to all prisoners as it may drop the cost to the taxpayers. Taxpayers saving might allow other things to be done that could also further benefit the taxpayers and everyone who lives or works in prison.

13 - Consequential Impact on Family

The consequences to children when the support of a parent is lost to prison can be substantial. It seems there are at least as many children impacted by incarceration as there are prisoners in lockup.

Growing up is not smooth for children but growing up with a loss of parental support can really shake things up. If the parent who is away was the breadwinner for the family, then there can be the complication of financial loss as well.

A day with dad could be a break for Mom.

Prisoner spouses of both sexes endure a lot of stress because of circumstances, and every bit of stress reduction can be beneficial to the greater community. The author of this book has been writing about reducing life struggles for many years and has a whole free website dedicated to it at http://www.StressReleaseCoach.com.

Laptop workers programs could eventually make a significant impact on jurisprudence change and the community because of:

1. Improving the lives and motivations of the prisoners.

2. Reducing Risk to prison or detention staff by preventing consequences by allowing more normal family interaction.

3. Motivating idea possibilities throughout the facility.

4. Creating hope and joy by providing a bit of consideration for everybody.

5. Family circuit integration for children.

6. Happier children are attending public schools.

7. Reduce the acting out of children because of unstable family units.

Risk
Of
Success
Ahead

Security concerns would need to be addressed up front, but segmentation could go a long way to securing the space and providing optimal success potential for all.

Nothing Ventured!

Nothing Gained!

16 - Wrap Up

If we want things to be different, we need to open our minds to all possibilities to attain the kind of changes that we would like to see manifest. After we find the ideas, we need to share our perspectives so that others may consider them.

There once was a bank in Philadelphia that had the saving "Wishing won't do it, Saving will."

I think that Wishing Won't do it, but thinking, sharing, assessing, planning, teaming, cooperating, re-thinking, and persistence will.

 I believe that the ideas needed are out there but need to be shared, considered and supported.

I wrote a series of books about that titled:
Prison Possibilities Dialogue Series: Concept
Prison Possibilities Dialogue Series: Volume 2 Dialogues
Prison Possibilities Dialogue Series: Volume 3 Dialogues
Prison Possibilities Dialogue Series: Volume 4 Dialogues
Prison Possibilities Dialogue Series: Volume 5 Dialogues

I share the invitation at http://angelraphaelspeaks.com/prison-possible/

I would love to have you participate in changing the reality of prison for those inside and the other 37 million or so people who are impacted indirectly and also the taxpayers.

May all who read this be blessed AND SO IT IS!

For
Considering
These
Ideas

Ever

It Does Not Help Prayer Still Does!

Resource: http://Create-A-Prayer.com

19 - Books Category Resources at www.Amazon.com

Distant Healing (or Mail List) e-mail mikewann@voicenet.com

Veterans Healing Six Pack plus 2
http://angelraphaelspeaks.com/healing-books/veterans/

PTSD Power Pack
http://angelraphaelspeaks.com/healing-books/ptsd/

Angel Raphael Speaks Series & Other Angel Books
http://angelraphaelspeaks.com/

Reiki
http://angelraphaelspeaks.com/healing-books/reiki/

Children
http://angelraphaelspeaks.com/healing-books/children/

Emergency Medical Kindness
http://angelraphaelspeaks.com/healing-books/emergency-medical-kindness/

Cancer
http://angelraphaelspeaks.com/healing-books/cancer/

Addictions
http://angelraphaelspeaks.com/healing-books/addictions/

Miscellaneous Healing
http://angelraphaelspeaks.com/healing-books/misc-healing/

Prison Books - 50+ Prison Books
http://angelraphaelspeaks.com/prison-books/

20 - Angels Please Prayers

Addict's

Angels of Healing Selected
Help Me to Stay Directed
Come To Me From The Sky
I Am Ready to Succeed Not Try
If I Don't Invite You In
I Might Not Win
I Have Been Lost For Too Long
Help Me To Stay Strong

Alcoholic's

Angels of Healing On High
Help Me to Stay Dry
Come To Me From The Sky
I Am Ready to Succeed Not Try
If I Don't Invite You In
I Might Not Win
I Have Been Lost For Too Long
Help Me To Stay Strong

From

http://AngelRaphaelSpeaks.com/AAAAAAA/
The Link Above Has the Core Messages from the book on drop-down pages.

21 - Private Channeling

Angel Raphael Speaks a series of free messages that are channeled through Reverend Mike Wanner for the Highest good and Highest Healing of all concerned.

Many questions arise about Reverend Mike doing private channeling, and he does help with that so E-mail him.

Reverend Mike is available worldwide as a psychic channel, emotional release facilitator, spiritual energy practitioner & teacher, and public speaker. He looks forward to meeting you soon! Email - mikewann@voicenet.com 215-342-1270

PRIVATE SPIRITUAL READINGS/channelings or Spiritual Healing Sessions: Telephone or in person.

Rev. Mike is available for individual, intuitive one-on-one sessions with you, his Guide Family, and your Guides. He helps by offering clarity on emotional situations about your life, your purpose, your spirituality, and your release of stuffed emotions and cellular memory.

Connect to the love of your Guides today!

For more information, Please visit

http://angelraphaelspeaks.com/channel/

22 - Reverend Mike Wanner

Rev. Mike Wanner started his spiritual and ministerial studies with Reiki in 1993 and had studied seven styles of Reiki in the U.S., Japan, Canada, Denmark and Australia. He is certified to teach. He became certified to teach Integrated Energy Therapy in 1999 and co-taught the first IET class of the new Millennium. Mike began dowsing in 2001.

Ordained as an Interfaith Minister of the Circle of Miracles Ministry and a Metaphysical Minister of the International Metaphysical Ministry, Rev. Mike practices and teaches spiritual energy therapies in the Philadelphia Area.

Rev. Mike holds ministerial degrees from the University of Metaphysics and the University of Sedona. He is a Pastoral Care Associate at Jefferson - Frankford Hospital. He taught at the National Academy of Massage Therapy and Health Sciences.

Rev. Mike was a faculty member of the Medical Mission Sister's Center for Human Integration's School of Integrated Body/Mind Therapies in Fox Chase, Philadelphia, PA for twelve years.

For a complete Biography, Please visit

http://ReverendMikeWanner.com/Bio

www.ingramcontent.com/pod-product-compliance
Lightning Source LLC
Chambersburg PA
CBHW071203220526
45468CB00003B/1141